Frank Lloyd Wright
AT A GLANCE

EARLY YEARS

Frank Lloyd Wright
AT A GLANCE

EARLY YEARS

Doreen Ehrlich

PRC

This edition first published in 2002 by
PRC Publishing Ltd,
64 Brewery Road, London N7 9NT
A member of the Chrysalis Group plc

Distributed in the U.S. and Canada by:
Sterling Publishing Co., Inc.
387 Park Avenue South
New York, NY 10016

ISBN 1 85648 630 3

Printed and bound in China

Page iii: Drafting room interior. The drafting room is an octagonally roofed two-story
structure. Its octagon on a cube shape recalls Wright's early childhood experience of
the Froebel Gifts. Wright's dramatic and radical design includes a balcony suspended
on great iron chains, a feat of architectural engineering, which made both maximum
use of limited space and provided an impressive demonstration of Wright's ability to
design working environments. The dramatic skylight and side windows provide ample
light for an architectural practice, while the carved texts are very much part of the
moral and aspirational work ethic of the period.

ACKNOWLEDGMENTS
The publisher wishes to thank Simon Clay for taking all the photography in this book,
    including the photographs on the front and back covers, with the following exceptions:
The images on pages 14 and 15, the Froebel "Gifts", appear courtesy of The Froebel
    Archive for Childhood Studies, University of Surrey, England.
The photographs on pages 51, 52 and 53 appear courtesy of Paul Rocheleau.
The photograph on the back cover (top) appears courtesy of © Bettmann/Corbis.

CONTENTS

INTRODUCTION

Although Frank Lloyd Wright, born in 1867 and living to 92, is regarded as one of the 20th century's greatest architects, his fundamental ideas and beliefs were formed at the end of the 19th century. In *An Autobiography*, Wright wrote with characteristic directness: "Early in life, I had to choose between honest arrogance and hypocritical humility. I chose the former and have seen no occasion to change." Such boundless self-confidence, together with Wright's lifelong desire to seek harmony with nature in his work, is essentially of the late 19th century. His philosophy should be seen in the context of such key thinkers as Ralph Waldo Emerson (1802–82) and Henry David Thoreau (1817–62), whose ideas formed part of Wright's formative years, and from which he was to draw on throughout his long life. They helped him develop a view of architecture that took nature, and organic forms for its models.

Wright's young adulthood in Wisconsin was marked by the fact that his father, William Cary Wright, who was a preacher and a musician, vanished without trace when he was only 18. William Wright's love of music and its performance, particularly Bach and Beethoven, was his only legacy to his son. His father's abandonment was to sadly foreshadow Wright's desertion of his wife, Catherine, and their six children 24 years later.

It is however clear that the decisive influence on Wright as a child had always been his mother, Anna Lloyd-Jones Wright, who had the highest ambitions for her only son. The Lloyd-Jones family, who were farmers, were essentially of their time in their dedication to self-improvement, and to education. One of Frank Lloyd Wright's earliest buildings was the first Hillside Home School of 1887, a progressive, coeducational establishment run by two of his maternal aunts, near Spring Green, Wisconsin. The charming Romeo and Juliet Windmill, which served the essential purpose of bringing water to the original school, still stands.

RIGHT: Plaque at the entrance doors of the Frank Lloyd Wright studio complex. The entrance to Wright's practice on Chicago Avenue, built as an addition to the original 1889 house in 1895, is quite separate from that of the house. It is approached through a loggia and this striking name plaque with its elegant lettering and distinctive device of a circle within a square is set into the brickwork of the entrance door. Richard Bock sculpted the plaque to drawings by Wright. Bock also provided the distinctive sculptural decoration of the studio facade.

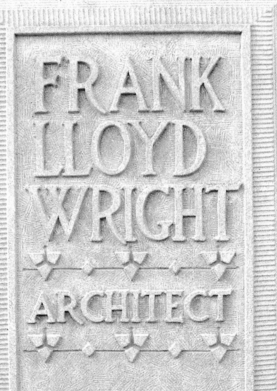

FRANK
LLOYD
WRIGHT

ARCHITECT

ABOVE: Frank Lloyd Wright Studio frontage on Chicago Avenue. The striking and dramatic practice frontage was crucial in establishing the young architect's credentials, and providing an important presence in the burgeoning and progressive suburb of Oak Park. The stepped frontage and entrance loggia, with its grand sculptures and bas-reliefs, acts as a centerpiece to the whole design, linking the reception hall to the library, and the octagonal drafting room.

Anna, who was of direct Welsh descent, took the motto of her family, "Truth against the world," and emphasized its importance to her only son. She was convinced from his earliest years that he was destined to become a great architect. Anna was much impressed by the Froebel system of kindergarten teaching, but lacked the means to attain it. Nevertheless, she provided her son with the teaching tools of the system, which used the basic forms of nature, irreducible geometric shapes in both two and three dimensions, the so-called "gifts." His childhood experience of the "gifts" had a profound influence on Wright's work throughout his life, as he later acknowledged: "...the modular system that has been the back of every design I ever made."

Froebel's system is dependent on learning by doing, and the child learns the fundamental laws of nature by working with simple wooden blocks, and brightly colored cardboard shapes. Organic forms drawn from nature are reduced to abstract shapes. The influence of this can be perceived in such a design as the barrel-vaulted playroom Wright was to build for his own children in 1895, and in the steep roofs and jutting eaves of the houses for some of his earliest clients. The most striking influence of the Froebel Gifts, however, may perhaps be seen in the Romeo and Juliet Windmill mentioned earlier, which was originally constructed in 1896 and supplied water to his maternal aunts' Hillside Home School. It may be read as a system of interlocking diamond and octagonal forms drawn directly from the blocks. Wright's choice of these forms, taken from his childhood education, for the windmill was particularly appropriate. He may well have been further influenced by the fact that his wife Catherine, along with other progressive parents at Oak Park, also used the Froebel Gifts as learning tools.

As Froebel's principles were to remain with Wright, so too would the influence of Emerson's philosophy with which it might be compared. The young overtly confident Wright may well have identified with Emerson's teaching that: "The intellect pierces the form, overleaps the wall, detects intrinsic likeness between remote things and reduces all things to a few principles."

In conventional terms, however, Wright had very little formal education as an architect. He completed just two semesters in engineering at the University of Wisconsin, while working in his professor's office, before he left to join the firm of J. Lynan Silsbee in Chicago. This was a post he obtained through a family connection, a strategic move that was to decide his future.

At the time, Chicago was in the midst of an unprecedented building boom, following the fire of 1871 that almost entirely destroyed its downtown area. Wright managed to secure a position in the leading architectural firm of Adler and Sullivan, where he trained from 1888–1893. Louis Sullivan was to become Wright's "lieber Meister," and his philosophy of architecture was to remain with Wright throughout his long life.

In 1889, Sullivan was also to provide crucial financial support for his young apprentice in the form of a loan of $5,000. This enabled the 22 year old to begin building what was originally a modest six-room bungalow for his wife and growing family at Oak Park.

During the years of Wright's apprenticeship with the firm, Sullivan and his

ABOVE: William H. Winslow house. The asymmetrical nature of the rear facade of the building is made clear from the air, as is the influence of the irreducible forms of the wooden blocks, known as the Froebel Gifts, which were an influential part of Wright's early education. The geometrical forms of the octagonal stair tower and semi-circular conservatory contrast with the symmetry of the main facade, and cannot be seen from the front. Only the centrally placed chimney above the "sacred hearth," which seems to strengthen the harmonious symmetry and balance of the frontage, is visible from the street.

partner, Dankmar Adler, were commissioned to design one of their most distinctive and radical buildings, the 13-story, metal-framed Chicago Stock Exchange. The centerpiece, the two-story trading room, has been reconstructed in the Art Institute of Chicago, where it provides an invaluable resource for the understanding of Sullivan's famous dictum "form follows function," and its influence on the work of his most famous follower. The vibrant, naturalistic color scheme of the room's design, which employs a system of painted stencils in no less than 57 different colors in 15 related and repeating organic patterns, is enhanced by the natural light from art glass skylights. The skylights repeat the motifs of the overall design, and create the idea of a verdant space in the midst of the bustling new city.

The idea of creating an inward-looking space, or "vista within" removed from exterior circumstance, was related to one of Wright's most influential objectives, that of an "organic architecture." Wright translated Sullivan's work from major public buildings, such as the Chicago Stock Exchange, or the vast and technologically advanced Auditorium building, and brought it to the private domain. The Adler and

RIGHT: Detail of a window in the Blossom house. Throughout the house the art glass is both subtle, and refined in its detail. Its forms show Wright breaking away from the floriated motifs of Louis Sullivan to geometric patterns of simple, irreducible shapes as is shown in this example. Much of the glass in the house is clear, achieving its decorative effect through the pattern of the caming. This example has restrained elements of color, which enhance its subtlety.

Sullivan practice was so busy with major public commissions, in what was fast becoming a showcase city, that domestic work commissions were in the main entrusted to their chief draftsman, as Wright was soon to become, while the partners retained overall supervision over more important commissions such as the Charnley residence.

Wright's experiments with the radical reworking of domestic space began in this way while he was working out his apprenticeship, and they continued through the "bootleg" commissions he obtained on the side while he was still working for Adler and Sullivan that would eventually lead to his departure from the practice. Many of his early works carry his characteristic stamp, albeit in embryonic form, in the detail of their interior planning, while the exteriors express the current interest in various forms of eclectic revival, from the Colonial style of the Blossom house to the Tudor elevation of the Moore residence.

In his mature work Wright was concerned with the breaking down of the conventional "box" of room spaces in the average domestic interior, and achieving spatial continuity by treating wall surfaces simply, and in as unbroken a manner as was feasible. This was a process that can be observed in the design of his own home and studio complex at Oak Park, where he was free to put his ideas into practice.

However, even in such an early building as the Blossom house, he can be seen to be attempting to open up the flow of spaces in internal areas, and dissolving the boundaries, where appropriate, between the building and its surrounding context. He wanted to achieve in practice what he described in words as, "vista without, vista within."

In the interests of regarding the whole interior space as an integral unit, Wright believed that doors and other openings should be conceived as part of an integrated structure, and that all necessary fittings, and indeed as much furniture as was practicable, should be built in. Wright wanted each home design to be unique and express the individuality of its owner, in his words emphasizing that: "Simplicity and repose are the qualities that measure the true value of any work of art."

This quality of repose sought by Wright in the design of domestic interiors is present from the beginning of his commissioned work, such as his first independent work, the William H. Winslow house. Clients, such as Winslow, required that their homes were all that their workplaces were not; a characteristic that is part of the architectural and design history of the late 19th-century suburb in both America and Europe. The male domain of the workplace was reached by railway—Oak Park is ten miles west of Chicago and was well served by commuter lines in Wright's time, while the female domain of the home was conceived as a place apart from that as "the house beautiful."

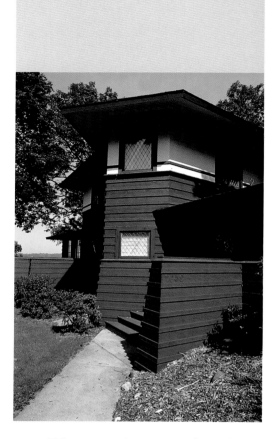

ABOVE: Wallis summer residence. Henry Wallis owned a real estate business, and commissioned Wright to design him a summer house at Delavan Lake, Wisconsin, on one of the several plots he was selling to Oak Park residents, such as himself, who wanted a holiday home. The house is an early instance of Wright's use of the module system later used for the Prairie and Usonian houses, in this case the module is 39in. (99cm).

ABOVE RIGHT: The Charnley house, Chicago. This residence shows Wright's early promise while still under the influence and supervision of Sullivan.

Wright shared the lifestyle of his clients, and understood their needs. While he was always to maintain a professional base in thriving downtown Chicago, before setting up his own architectural practice in Oak Park, he too had divided his working day between the center of the city, and the tranquillity of the dormitory suburb. While he and Catherine were early enthusiasts for such public cultural events as the subscription concerts of the Chicago Symphony, he understood that spaces for entertaining and music-making in the home were an important part of social life.

Many of Wright's early clients were self-made men like Wright himself, men he was to characterize later as having, "unspoiled instincts and untainted ideals." His first independent client, William Winslow, shared an interest in both science and art with Wright, and Wright's business interest in Winslow's prismatic lighting process enabled him to enlarge the home and studio complex at Oak Park. In these early years, Wright's links with his clients at Oak Park and River Forest were further strengthened by their common interest in music and music-making, which Wright believed "blossomed on the same stem" as architecture. Both were in his view, "sublimated mathematics... Instead of the musician's staff and intervals, the architect has a modular system as the framework of the design."

Wright's own home and studio complex was used experimentally as a forcing ground for his ideas to be put into practice, and both are far more advanced than the homes built for clients of the same period. The rift with Sullivan appears to have been caused by Wright's "moonlighting" on such commissions. In general the more radical ideas may be seen in the interiors, where Wright felt freer to experiment.

Wright parted company with Sullivan in 1893, the year of the World's Columbian Exposition, which brought 27 million visitors to the "White City" in Chicago during the course of the summer. By then Wright was part of an enlightened circle at the forefront of the city's development in the midst of an unprecedented building boom. The Oak Park and River Forest clients shared interests and ambitions with Wright, which transcended the usual client/architect relationship. They like him were bringing up young families in new territory in circumstances particular to the time and the place. The designs of the houses he built

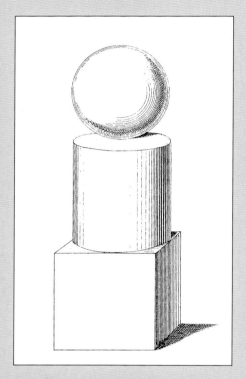

ABOVE: Example of the Froebel Gifts. The simple wooden blocks of irreducible forms were given to Frank Lloyd Wright as a child by his mother, and were to form a key influence on his work throughout his life.

FAR RIGHT: The Froebel Gifts, illustrated in *The Kindergarten Guide* published in New York, 1886. The illustration shows the First Gift : a box containing six balls (top left), and games with one ball (figs. 1-8); and the Second Gift: a box showing a sphere, cylinder and cube suspended (top right), and games, (figs. 1-6 below).

for them had to accommodate the extremes of temperature in Chicago and its environs, and rendered the comfort factor of buildings a crucial concern.

While employed by Sullivan and Adler, Wright had worked on such technologically advanced buildings as the vast Auditorium building, which used advances in lighting, acoustic technology, and air conditioning to an unprecedented degree, making it a truly modern building. Wright was later to put such experience to good use in his public buildings, but while his practice was confined to domestic commissions he nonetheless was well aware of the importance of ensuring his clients' physical comfort. The glare of the Illinois summers was accommodated by the overhang of the eaves of many of the houses, which enabled him to use decorative art glass to brilliant effect. The built-in furniture, which begins to feature in some of the early houses, was able to accommodate carefully placed, boxed-in steam radiators, helping control temperature in the extremes of the Chicago winters. Wright's key concept of "the sacred hearth" that often had its own cosy inglenook, and which stood at the heart of family life, was augmented with central heating throughout the living space.

In these earlier years, Wright can be seen to be experimenting with the latest technologies, while working through and rejecting the revivals of classical styles employed by some contemporary architects. Apart from his own home and studio, the major domestic work of this period, namely the William H. Winslow house in River Forest, presents a synthesis of what might be termed his early mature style in its simplification of forms, and particularly in its interior spaciousness, and sense of repose. Wright believed that the design of houses should signify the private domain; the idea of shelter. This was in contrast with public buildings, which needed to symbolize power and success in terms of height. To this end, as

Wright wrote later on, "the horizontal line is the line of domesticity...shelter should be the essential look of any dwelling." This radical concept, so essential to the design of the Prairie Houses, is first seen in the Winslow house. For the first time the house is made to seem an integral part of its setting. Wright achieves "the sense of shelter" in the long, low lines of the house, which make it seem at one with its site, and particularly by the central placing of the huge chimney, which serves the "sacred hearth," central to Wright's ideal of family life.

Other less radical domestic commissions of the time, built for clients who did not share Wright's ideas in the same way as Winslow, show Wright reworking currently fashionable historical styles into what might be termed abstract and pared down versions. For example, this can be seen by the Colonial Revival style of the Blossom house in 1893, or the "Gothic" vocabulary employed in the four huge gables that top the geometric facade of the Roloson apartments a year later. The "Tudor" vocabulary employed in the Nathan Moore

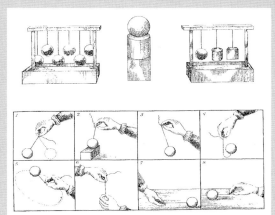

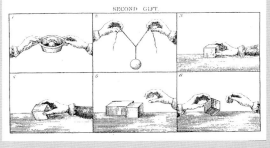

SECOND GIFT.

house was insisted on by the client, who told Wright: "I don't want you to give us anything like that house you did for Winslow. I don't want to go down the backstreets to my morning train to avoid being laughed at."

Wright's rejection of revivalism, and the break with the architectural past that this implied, was much influenced by Sullivan's dictum "form follows function," which found its most characteristic expression in the tall public buildings of Sullivan and the Chicago School.

Although Wright's work in this early period was almost entirely domestic, there is one great surviving exception, Unity Temple. It encapsulates many of Wright's ideas and practices, first explored in domestic spaces, in terms of a key public building that both serves the local community, and expresses the shared ethos of architect and congregation.

Unity Temple was a major commission for Wright's small studio in 1905. The original Unitarian Universalist church had burned down during a storm that same year, and the modest budget of only $60,000 necessitated the use of economic building materials. Wright's decision to use a solid masonry of concrete was

LEFT: Frank Lloyd Wright home: playroom looking west. The barrel-vaulted playroom is 15ft. (4.5m) high, and provides what is the first dramatic space of Wright's career with a new sense of spaciousness not felt in the earlier rooms of the house. The windows are at the height of a child, and adults must stoop to look out of them. This is an imaginative concept on Wright's part that extends to other features of the room, such as the overmantel mural, which took its theme from *The Arabian Nights*.

turned to brilliant effect, both in the esthetics of the design, and the practical need for a peaceful space on a heavily trafficked site. Wright regarded it as a watershed in his career.

Interviewed over 50 years after it was built, he reflected: "I think that was about the first time when the interior space began to come through as the reality of the building. When you sat in the Temple, you were sitting under a big concrete slab that let your eyes go out into the clouds on four sides. Then there were no walls with holes in them. You will notice that features were arranged against that interior space allowing a sense of it to come to the beholder wherever he happened to be. And I have been working on that thesis for a long time, because it was dawning on me when I built that the reality of the building did not consist in the walls and in the roof, but in this space within to be lived in."

Unity Temple, regarded as one of the icons of 20th-century architecture, continues to serve the Oak Park congregation, and is still owned by it. The building brought his architecture and ideas to a much wider public than the domestic commissions of the time, and is the only public building from his early career that is still in use.

2

CASE STUDIES

FRANK LLOYD WRIGHT HOME AND STUDIO

Home Constructed: 1889–1895   Studio Constructed: 1895–1906
Address: 951 Chicago Avenue, Oak Park, Illinois 60302.
Tours daily.

In 1888, Wright married Catherine Tobin, and with a loan of $5000 from his architectural mentor, Louis Sullivan, began building a house in the leafy Chicago suburb of Oak Park. The 22 year old architect was able to put his architectural principles into practice in what started out originally as a modest, six-room bungalow, which Wright added to and adapted over the next 20 years. A sizable studio, containing a drafting room, an office, and a library was later added to the house, and the complex became both home and working environment for the Wrights and their growing family.

Wright used both house and studio to experiment with ideas and their implementation, and the working out of his radical experiments with space and form were subject to the practicalities of day-to-day family life. It is clear that the young Wright used the house as a type of laboratory in which he both experimented with ideas, and experienced their reality before applying the lessons learned to his commissioned work for clients.

RIGHT: Interior of library. In late 19th-century American and European domestic architecture, the term "library" covered several functions. In the studio complex it is clear that the space provided a setting as a conference room for the practice and its clients, as well as acting as a library in the conventional sense of the word. The skylight and placing of the windows provide functional lighting that offers privacy and freedom from distraction.The purpose-built oak furniture and fixtures and careful placing of selected artifacts offer the ideal setting in which client and architect could confer.

The house is remarkable both in its use of materials—brick, oak, and glass in the main—and particularly in the innovative use of space in its modest interiors. The living room, for example, is remarkable in its open plan. It has a continuous stringcourse at ceiling height emphasizing the movement, continuity, and flow of the interior spaces one into another, so that the walls take on the appearance of screens. As Wright wrote in his paper of 1908 *In the Cause of Architecture*: "really there need be but one room, the living room … openings should occur as integral features of the structure and form, if possible its natural ornamentation." The door openings are wide, and the use of oak throughout provides warmth and visual continuity, as does the built-in seating.

The focal point of the living room is a brick-built hearth within a cosy inglenook. The idea of what Wright was to term "the sacred hearth," as the heart of the home and of family life, is seen in its clearest form here. The inglenook space could have floor-length curtains drawn about it to ensure greater privacy, while the carved text above the fireplace emphasizes the special status of the space. The entire living room space has an intimacy and integrated flow around the focal point of the hearth, which was to become such a marked feature of Wright's domestic work.

By 1895, the Wrights had four children and the domestic space was in obvious need of enlargement. Wright was able to fund additions to the home from the proceeds of his work with the Luxfer Prism Company, who produced a technologically advanced system of lighting for public spaces in the boom years of Chicago's rebuilding. The new dining room is a remarkably intimate space, distinguished by the manner in which it is lit. The windows of art glass are set high to ensure privacy and the diffusion of light throughout the room, and the ceiling has a fretwork screen of amber and gold glass that provides a subtle source of light and mirrors the shape of the dining table beneath it.

The whole space forms a "total environment," the precursor of many such spaces to come. Wright's desire for complete integration in the domestic interior even extended to designing dresses for his wife, which were quite different from contemporary fashions. There are at least two surviving photographs of Catherine wearing dresses of a strictly geometric cut, which corresponded to the angular design of the furnishings, and the rectilinear patterns of the art glass windows.

ABOVE: Living room seating area. The open flow of interior space around the central hearth, of which this is the earliest example to include living room, dining room and stairhall, was to become a key feature of Wright's desire for an "organic architecture." This drew its inspiration directly from nature. Here the sense of an uninterrupted flow of space is enhanced by the low ceiling and integrated built-in seating, while the leaded window glass provides the sense of privacy essential to the concept of Wright's "vista within," and to his ideal of family life.

The barrel-vaulted playroom which occupies the entire second floor of the new wing is 15ft. (4.5m) high, and is lit by an art glass skylight set in a wooden fretwork ceiling. The windows of the room are set at the height of a child, while adults must stoop to look out of them. This is an imaginative concept on Wright's part that extends to other features of the room, such as the stair-stepped balcony, scaled for children, and the splendid mural that takes its theme from *The Arabian Nights*.

Here the children put on performances for their parents and neighbors, and Catherine and other progressive parents used the Froebel Gifts, a series of irreducible geometric forms given to children in the form of blocks, as learning tools. The setting was particularly appropriate, as the design of the room can be seen to owe much to the Froebel Gifts, which had so enlightened Wright's own childhood.

RIGHT: North bedroom. Wright's desire for simplicity, and ornament that was organic and fully integrated into the whole is seen throughout the later additions to his house including the main bedroom. From the beginning of his career his philosophy of domestic design was to achieve a sense of repose in the family interior, as far removed from the stresses of the public domain as possible. Here these qualities are seen in the simplicity of the design, which had recently appeared in the work of William Morris and his followers in the English Arts and Crafts Movement. These are typified by the "honest" use of natural materials and the flow of natural light in a high-ceilinged space.

ABOVE: Forest Avenue elevation. While maintaining an office in Chicago for business meetings, Wright wanted to integrate his work and his family life in a setting removed from the strains of city life and in a calm environment close to nature. The modest bungalow was adapted to this purpose between 1895 and 1898. Though connected internally, the house entrance is on Forest Avenue and the studio has an entirely separate entrance on Chicago Avenue.

STUDIO

By 1895, with the proceeds from his work with the Luxfer Prism Company, which produced a technologically advanced system of lighting that brought natural light to public spaces before the widespread use of electricity, Wright decided to run his growing architectural practice from his home base at Oak Park. He began designing a showcase studio addition to the house, which he had begun building as a home for his wife and growing family six years before.

The studio complex forms a separate entity from the house. Although they are interconnected, each has a separate entrance, and a distinctive character of its own. Moving his practice from downtown Chicago to the affluent suburb, where most of his clients lived, was a decisive move, and one which Wright anticipated increasing his output by at least a third.

RIGHT: Living room fireplace and inglenook. For Wright the "sacred hearth" was the focal point of the domestic interior. Such focal points were to feature strongly throughout his domestic work, from the earliest houses to the modern interpretation of such a central feature at "Wingspread" (the Herbert F. Johnson house) and the Usonian houses half a century later. Here the fireplace has its own inglenook, which could be separated by curtains.

LEFT: Stork plaque at the entrance to the studio. Four such bas-reliefs decorate the piers of the loggia at the entrance to the studio complex on Chicago Avenue. Richard Bock, who was Wright's favored architectural sculptor, worked from detailed drawings by Wright, which still exist. The storks, which symbolize fertility, flank a ground plan of the Roman baths of Caracalla (A.D. 217) linking the young architect with the great architecture of the past, while the stylized oak leaves represent life. On Wright's annotated drawing for the plaques, he was to identify the storks as "wise birds," which may perhaps be a humorous reference to their mythical qualities.

TRUTH IS LIFE.

GOOD FRIEND, AROVND THESE
HEARTH-STONES SPEAK NO EVIL
WORD OF ANY CREATVRE.·.

a Use of natural materials: brick, stone, wood, glass, and plaster predominate here, and were used consistently throughout Wright's long career.

b Organic architecture: Wright aimed for a "sense of shelter" and for unity. The dominant horizontals are reinforced by the loggia and the enclosing brick wall, stressing the creative purpose of the studio and its integration with the home.

c Outward expression of interior space: the function of the studio is made clear by the large lighted spaces of the drafting room, while the chimney of the studio echoes the one in the home beyond, reinforcing the linked nature of the two.

d Use of geometric forms: the octagonal drafting room to the left and the library on the right are linked by the central loggia, and emphasized by triangular gables and rectangular chimneys.

e Organic ornament based on forms from nature: the ornamental details of the studio are a unified part of the facade and serve to declare its artistic function.

The burgeoning, architectural practice necessitated more working space for Wright and his assistants, as well as a suitably impressive space in which to receive clients and contractors. The complex of rooms demonstrates the radical development in Wright's thinking, which had accelerated rapidly in a short space of time. The experimental features introduced here were to be key to the development of the working environments, which were to form such a crucial part of Wright's later work from the Great Room of the Johnson Wax building to the Marin County Civic Center.

The studio has a grand and complex entranceway for clients, quite separate from the family part of the house. Whereas the house itself is dominated by a massive, sheltering, shingle-covered gable on the Forest Avenue facade, the studio complex on Chicago Avenue presents itself to the street as a series of vertical forms built of brick. A long, low loggia links the octagonal drafting room to the library, and the facade is embellished with sculptured plaques together with free-standing sculptures on top of the entrance piers.

The drafting room is the most dramatic of all the interior spaces, which are paneled throughout. Its octagonal balcony is suspended from the roof rafters by huge iron chains, and the entire space is suffused with natural light from bands of windows on each of the levels; an ideal and essential feature to an architectural

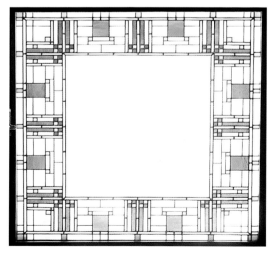

practice. The use of glass throughout the studio complex is remarkable in its sophistication, and is used for different purposes in each of the interior spaces. For example, the three spectacular art glass skylights of the studio reception room, where clients and contractors were received, is not simply

LEFT: Studio window. Wright's own private office in the studio at Oak Park is lit from above through a skylight with art glass such as this, providing a secluded retreat from the busy practice. Three windows form the focal point of the room, focusing the view through the clear plate glass at their centers. Wright believed that design should not compete with nature, but complement it, as it does here, and that "the view should stay severely put."

RIGHT: Studio reception hall. This dramatic space, directly beyond the entrance loggia had several functions. In addition to its primary purpose as a reception room for clients and contractors, the reception hall served as a link between the drafting room to the east, the octagonal library to the west, and Wright's own office. The tapestry-like patterns of the skylight glass add a sense of directional impulse between the spaces of the studio complex. This provides richly patterned toplighting which maximizes the effect of what is a relatively small space.

an integrated decorative feature, but also serves the purpose of linking the drafting room, Wright's office, and the library. Wright's own private office has the most spectacular art glass in the whole home and studio complex at Oak Park. Before him as he worked was a triptych of windows formed of bright green and amber glass in a design constructed of squares, rectangles, and bars. They were designed to frame the view while safeguarding privacy by keeping the view from the window, as Wright wrote "severely put."

The studio complex, and the adjoining house were completed by June 1898, establishing Wright's significant architectural presence in Oak Park. Until his flight from Oak Park in 1909, the site became the center of Wright's enterprise, and a powerhouse for his ideas, which were transmitted throughout the United States and Europe. Designs for some 162 buildings were produced from the modest complex of buildings, to which it has been estimated Wright made changes on average at least once every six months.

JAMES CHARNLEY HOUSE

Constructed: 1891
Address: 1365 North Astor Street, Chicago, Illinois 60610.
Tours available.

The architectural practice of Adler and Sullivan, to which Wright was apprenticed for five years, was in the main occupied with major public buildings. These included the Auditorium building in Chicago of 1889, and the 13-story, metal-framed Chicago Stock Exchange on which the young Wright must have worked when he first entered the practice. Such prestigious public buildings were the means of making the Adler and Sullivan practice the busiest as well as the most famous in Chicago in the midst of an unprecedented building boom. As a result, domestic commissions were not usually within the remit of the partners, and were often given to their chief draftsman to work on as overtime. Wright's contribution to the Charnley house can never be firmly established, but there are some elements of the imposing building that would suggest the hand of the fledgling architect. In later life, Wright was to claim to have been the principal designer of what he termed this "first modern building," although the preponderance of Sullivanesque elements in the design would seem to contradict this, and the truth will never be established with any clarity. However, it may well be that Sullivan gave Wright the major part of the design for the Charnley house on Astor Street. He had enormous trust in his young apprentice, enough to commission him to design a vacation house for himself, as well as one for his mother, and another for his partner, Adler.

RIGHT: Detail of second and third floor elevation. The detailed treatment of the Charnley house decoration is remarkable for its elegance and refined use of materials, notably brick, fine stone, and cast bronze. The bronze decorative elements are geometric, while the decoration of the loggia offers a restrained and geometric variant of Sullivan-style motifs, wholly in keeping with the harmony, symmetry, and balance of the whole facade.

If it was mostly Wright's design, it was significant and astonishing in the work of an architect not yet 24 to create the grand exterior elevation that commands its city center site with such authority. Its dignity sets it apart from the buildings that surround it, despite, or perhaps because of, its markedly lower height. Its neighbors are built in a range of different historical styles that were then in fashion. In the materials of its construction too, the Charnley house is set apart from its neighbors. The two upper stories are built of Roman brick, recessed above the centrally placed entrance to form a decorative loggia, which gives the building an air of classical grandeur, as does the base of smoothly finished ashlar stone. Later, Wright in *An Autobiography* recognized the importance of the building: "In this Charnley city-house on Astor Place I first sensed the definitely decorative value of the plain surface, that is to say, of the flat plane as such."

It is this smooth, flush surface, and the lack of projecting moldings on the entire facade, which help make the exterior of the Charnley house such an extraordinary work. The austerity of the facade, and the horizontality of the design as a whole mark out the Charnley house from its contemporary neighbors, which were designed to reflect a whole variety of historical revival styles. In contrast, the building appears extraordinarily modern in idea and execution.

ABOVE: Charnley house carved decoration. The interior decoration of the Charnley house is rich and complex, using motifs derived from organic forms reminiscent of those used by Louis Sullivan in his great public buildings of the time, such as the Auditorium building and the trading floor of the Chicago Stock Exchange.

RIGHT: Carved newel post of central stair. The grand oak central staircase, which is lit by a skylight, is the dominant feature of the interior of Charnley house. The prominent newel post is carved in the style of Louis Sullivan, using motifs derived from leaf and plant forms.

The interior plan and disposition of rooms mirrors the facade, which is in three parts. It has a central stair hall, which goes through the entire height of the building, and is suffused with natural light from a skylight; a characteristic form of lighting seen in future domestic and public Wright buildings. The central staircase is broad and gentle in its incline, and has a distinctive baluster and staircage of thin, flat oak spindles reminiscent of that used in the William H. Winslow house. The austere geometry of all levels of the central stair hall is in strictest contrast to the exuberance of the floriate decoration throughout the house, notably on the newel post, and the inner front door. Such decoration is clearly related to the interiors of Adler and Sullivan's great public buildings of the time, notably the Auditorium and the trading floor of the Chicago Stock Exchange, now preserved in the Art Institute of Chicago. The building was restored in 1988, and in 1995 it became the headquarters of the Society of Architectural Historians.

LEFT: View of the stair hall. The three-story space is lit by a skylight and the oak staircase is both broad and spacious and gentle in its incline. The thin spindles of the staircage are a restrained and geometric contrast to the exuberance of the filigree decoration of the stairwell and of the newel post that echoes similar decorative devices in such Sullivan designs as the Auditorium building. In general the centrality and lightness of the stair hall space as a whole may be said to prefigure several subsequent Wright buildings, both public and private.

RIGHT: Entrance facade and loggia. The entrance facade is constructed of Roman brick and finely finished ashlar stone, giving it an air of austere grandeur enhanced by the second floor loggia with its classical columns and elegant frieze.

WARREN MCARTHUR HOUSE

Constructed: 1892
Address: 4852 Kenwood Avenue, Chicago, Illinois 60615.

The design for the Warren McArthur house, another "bootleg" commission, was undertaken while Wright was "moonlighting" from his five-year apprenticeship with Adler and Sullivan. It was published under the name of Cecil C. Corbin, with whom Wright had worked with while in the office of his former architectural master, the then fashionable architect, J. Lyman Silsbee.

The McArthur house occupies the site adjacent to the Blossom house and its exterior is also eclectic in style, although in this case the elevation might be classified as Dutch Colonial by reason of its steep gambrel roof and dormers. However, the treatment of the outside walls is unusual, constructed of Roman brick, while the casement windows, that favored form of Wright's, are set in a band of brown plaster. The house is large, and has a spacious and well lit stairwell, five bedrooms on the second floor, and a barrel-vaulted room on the third floor, which anticipates by some time the barrel-vaulted playroom at Wright's own house.

It is, moreover, in the interior design that the young Wright can be seen to radically break away from his past. The hearth is placed centrally between the entrance hall, and the dining room with a free passage of space on either side. This anticipates by almost two decades the fully evolved Prairie Style groundplan of the Robie house, where the fireplace stands free of the side walls. In the remodeling of the house, which took

RIGHT: Dining room. The remodeling of the dining room, completed in 1902, marks a radical departure in Wright's work. The house is built on a narrow site, and is oriented with its short side towards the street. As an embellishment to the original house, Wright was commissioned to design such fixtures as the Californian oak woodwork that includes a wall-length sideboard with art glass doors, much of the furniture, and the entrance doors that employ the same arrowhead design as the elaborate sideboard fixture.

place shortly after the turn of the century, Wright was to further set his stamp on the house by being commissioned to design the paneling and many of the wooden fixtures, and even some of the furniture. The dining room has the most elaborate fixtures, and the designs for the impressive built-in buffet, and glazed interior doors give some taste of his later fully integrated interiors, and his ideal of an "organic architecture." It is the first time that Wright was able to put into practice his ideas for a fully integrated interior, apart of course from the design of his own house at Oak Park. The lines of the oak wainscoting of the hall, and built-in furniture throughout the house echo one another in the strictly geometric motifs of their design, which owe nothing to Sullivan's influence in its forms.

In addition, the interior design of the house represents a pivotal point in Wright's use of art glass, particularly in the glass of the dining room, which was almost certainly remodeled by 1902. The glass-making firm of Giannini and Hilgart, favored collaborators of Wright in his Chicago period, and also responsible for the superb art glass ensembles at the 1901 Frank Thomas house at Oak Park, provided the glass of the dining room— the finest glass in the house.

The high point of the design for the McArthur house, the dining room, represents a radical breakaway from the richly decorative style of Wright's master. There is no trace of Sullivan's curvilinear decorative style, the decorative motifs are rectilinear and abstract in form, employing an arrowhead design throughout the house, which is somewhat similar to that used in the Frank Thomas house. A feathery arrowhead

RIGHT: McArthur house dining room and buffet. The art glass at the McArthur house is particularly elaborate in the dining room remodeling of 1902. This represents a pivotal point in Wright's use of art glass, a change which is in strict contrast to the austerity of the glass designs of the adjoining Blossom house .

design is also employed in the upper register of the doors of the dining room, and repeated and elaborated upon in the sideboard fixture. The importance of the dining room remodeling in Wright's early work may be seen in the fact that it was featured in the March 1904 *The House Beautiful* as "A Yellow Drawing Room," where it helped further his reputation for innovative and elegant interior design.

RIGHT: On an adjacent lot to the Blossom house and built in the same year, the McArthur house might appear to be another exercise in a period revival style, in this case Dutch Colonial by reason of its steeply hipped roof and dormers. As with the Blossom house, however, the historicism of the period style conceals some interesting innovative details. These include the dado of Roman brick surmounted by a brown plaster band into which the casement windows are set. The use of casement windows is more extensive than in previous houses, anticipating Wright's widespread use of the form in subsequent designs.

GEORGE BLOSSOM HOUSE

Constructed: 1892

Address: 4858 Kenwood Avenue, Chicago, Illinois 60615.

The George Blossom residence is one of several "bootleg" commissions designed while the young Wright was working for the partnership of Louis Sullivan and Dankmar Adler. Under the terms of his five-year contract they expected the young architect to devote his time exclusively to them. When it became clear that the 25 year old apprentice had been "moonlighting" on such houses as the Blossom residence, and the neighboring Warren McArthur house, Wright's tenure with the practice was summarily terminated.

The two-storied house is one of several exercises by Wright in an historical mode, and is New England Colonial Revival in form with a symmetrical front, and clapboard siding. The house is in sharp contrast to Wright's later design for the adjoining coach house of 1907, which is built on the long, low lines of the typical Prairie design. The revived Colonial style was just becoming fashionable in the Midwest, and the Blossom house has the classical portico, fan-lighted doorway and butter-yellow clapboards so characteristic of this architectural fashion. As an experiment with a current mode of building, the house may still be seen to have

RIGHT: Dining room. The formal dining area opens out of the living room, and as with the living room fireplace and inglenook, it too is framed within an arch to provide a "vista within" the interior space. The dining room windows are set in a curve in a pattern of bordered squares, which evoke New England Colonial designs. The windows are outward-opening casements, a form Wright considered essential to his concept of the spatial relationship between the interior of the house and "the vista without."

some quirky Wrightian features. Not least of these is the massive chimney of Roman brick, and the fact that the conventional classical cornice is replaced by the sharp projection of the eaves of the flattened hip roof.

Wright here uses the conventional form of sash window, a type he much disliked, terming them "guillotine windows," but these are unconventionally oblong in form. Wright was obviously able to declare his own preferences in the most distinguished room of the house, the elegant dining room, where the striking layout was centered on a series of subtly designed casement windows that opened outwards.

Vistas were central to Wright's philosophy of architecture, even at this early stage in his career. The idea of casements opening to the outside world required a radical rethinking of the traditional casement, which opened onto the inward space, rather than, as with the dining room windows of the Blossom residence, opening outwards. The square forms of the design resemble the motifs employed in the architecture of the Colonial period, and the window bay seems to be a continuous band of light that appears both as an extension of the room space, and marks its relation to the exterior world. The dining room is the most interesting of the

interior spaces, showing the young architect's search for change, while other elements of the design, not least the curvilinear designs of the entrance hall, also show his growing confidence as a designer. The design also shows the influence of

LEFT: Detail of window glass. Throughout the Blossom house the art glass is both subtle and refined in its detail. Its forms show Wright breaking away from the floriated motifs of Louis Sullivan to geometric patterns of simple, irreducible shapes as in this example. Much of the glass in the house is clear, achieving its effect through the pattern of the caming. This example has restrained elements of color, which help to enhance its subtlety.

ABOVE: Entrance front. A facade of elegant symmetry, the entrance is marked by a curved portico and the fan-lighted entrance door is reached by a flight of steps. The classicism of the facade is enhanced by Wright's choice of Ionic columns, the most elegant of the orders of classical architecture. An exercise in the newly fashionable New England Colonial style, the house has interesting features that show Wright's increasing independence from accepted norms, such as the unexpected placing of the massive chimney and the shallow hip roof.

his mentor Sullivan's teaching that all ornament should be integral, and make use of geometric forms drawn from nature. It has been noted that other elements of the design may well derive from the major influence of Wright's childhood, the Froebel Gifts that were introduced to him as part of his early education. This is particularly clear in the patterns of the glass of the hall, where the caming that contains the clear glass is geometric in form, almost certainly created with a compass as advised in the 11th Froebel Gift.

Wright was always to acknowledge his early influences, and 40 years later, looking back on his early work in *An Autobiography*, was very clear in his classification of such early houses as the Blossom residence. He described them as: "... buildings all characterized to a certain extent by the Sullivanian idiom, at least in detail. I couldn't invent the terms of my own overnight. At that time there was nothing in sight that might be helpful." The Blossom residence remains one of the most interesting of Wright's early buildings; its design creating a sense of harmony and repose, albeit in a historical mode.

RIGHT: Living room fireplace and inglenook. Wright's concept of the "sacred hearth" was central to his domestic design, as he believed it should be the focal point of the home and family life. Here the fireplace is enclosed within a cosy inglenook, with fitted seating and cupboards above the fireplace, which is faced with olive tiles. The fireplace is the focal point of the living room and is framed from the anteroom within a double banded wooden archway, providing a "vista within," a crucial feature of Wright's interior design esthetic from the beginning of his career. The staircase can be seen on the right through the thin spindles of the staircage.

WILLIAM H. WINSLOW HOUSE

Constructed: 1893
Address: 515 Auvergne Place, River Forest, Illinois 60305.

After the rift with Louis Sullivan and the establishment of his new architectural practice in Oak Park, Wright was soon to receive his first significant independent domestic commission from William H. Winslow in the neighboring suburb of River Forest. Winslow, like many of Wright's early clients shared his business interests and lifestyle. Like Wright, Winslow was a self-made man, whose interests embraced both science and art. Winslow and his brother Francis ran a large, and technologically advanced bronze and iron casting foundry in Chicago. They were also inventors, advancing their own industrial processes, which included the prismatic electroglazing process that resulted in the Luxfer Prism, for which Wright produced designs. The proceeds enabled him to build the studio complex at Oak Park, and extend the family part of the house.

Winslow's electroglazing process was a vital element in Wright's early work, enabling him to produce the innovative "glass screens" of windows, or toplighting, which are so distinctive a feature of his work at the time. The flat, rectilinear patterns made possible by the process, and the subdued tonalities of the glass palette chosen by Wright distinguish his work sharply from that of his contemporaries, rendering it distinctively modern. The Winslow brothers' interests also included typography, an interest shared with Wright, and the influential and lavish production of William C. Gannett's *The House Beautiful* was published by Winslow from his own press at River Forest.

RIGHT: View of stair tower facade. The rear elevation of the Winslow house is in contrast to the main facade, which is classical and balanced using cast concrete brick and stone. The prominent stair tower is octagonal in form, and is set asymmetrically into the design as a whole. Its most distinctive feature is the vertical line of windows, which are "Gothic" in form with medieval style tracery. The picturesque appearance is accentuated by the varied height of the roof lines, and the finely detailed brickwork.

With such a client, who allowed him unprecedented freedom, Wright was able to produce a startlingly innovative design, particularly for an architect of 26 who had left his "lieber Meister" Louis Sullivan, but two weeks before the designs were begun. The house is built of traditional organic materials— brick, cast concrete, and terra cotta—which were all used in Roman architecture, but here employed in a distinctly untraditional manner. The house is not only built from Roman materials, but is conceived in a classical manner. A harmonious, balanced facade is centered on a distinctive entranceway.

ABOVE: View into dining room from the living room. The Winslow house contains two central hearths, back to back beneath the central chimney that appears to pin the exterior to the ground and emphasize its broad horizontal lines. The arcaded inglenook, the most striking feature of the interior design, opens from the reception hall, while this smaller "sacred hearth" backs on to it, and forms the most prominent feature of the dining room.

RIGHT: View of hall arcade and inglenook. Three steps lead to the arcade, which houses the hearth. The hearth and inglenook are designed as the focal point of the entire building. The centrally placed hearth chimney indicates the importance of "the sacred hearth" when read from the outside. The columns of the arcade are slender and classical in form with carved capitals, and elaborately decorated spandrels.

However, the front elevation distinguishes itself from its traditional neighbors by its roofline, which is low in pitch and projects beyond its eaves, and its use of color and materials. Dark brown terra cotta with a Sullivanesque frieze recalls plant forms at the upper levels, and gold-toned brick is used for the lower story. The harmony, symmetry, and balance of the front facade is in strictest contrast to the quirky rear elevation that has an octagonal stair tower, slender gothic-style windows, and angular lines of decorative brickwork.

The interior of the house is no less remarkable, particularly in its use of wood. The hall arcade is a most distinctive feature with its prominent fireplace and inglenook, and subtle use of lighting. Wright's "sacred hearth" here achieves an extraordinary centrality to the whole house, raised as it is on a podium of three steps placed facing the entrance door, and designed on a scale which makes the inglenook and hearth a virtually independent space. The elegance of the slender columns and classical capitals, which form the inglenook arcade, is enhanced by the carved decoration of the spandrels, and the frieze that has restrained floriate decoration containing heraldic motifs.

Elsewhere in the interior, the Winslow house can be seen to mark a watershed in Wright's career. This can be seen in the flow of its interior spaces, and the use of decoration in particular, which combines classical motifs, such as egg and dart plasterwork, with painted friezes, and the remarkable use of glass. The conservatory is particularly impressive, where the curved bay gives on to the "vista without" through a series of identical casement windows between columns. Each frames the view in an identical pattern of elegant abstract plant forms.

In *An Autobiography* 39 years later, Wright acknowledged the importance of the Winslow house in his career: "The Winslow house had burst on the view of that provincial suburb like the Prima Vera in full bloom. It was a new world to Oak Park and River Forest. That house became an attraction, far and near. Incessantly it was courted and admired. Ridiculed, too, of course. Ridicule is always modeled on the opposite side of that shield."

ABOVE: Conservatory windows. The conservatory is semi-circular in shape, and the design of the leaded glass is distinctive in form. Other parts of the house, notably the frieze and front door carving, demonstrate Wright's use of Sullivan's vocabulary of ornament, which was based on plant and foliage forms. For the conservatory windows, Wright appears to have derived the geometric shapes in part from the use of a compass, a practice recommended by his childhood education using the Froebel Gifts.

ISIDORE HELLER HOUSE

Constructed: 1896
Address: 5132 Woodham Avenue, Chicago, Illinois 60615

The Isidore Heller house is built on a restrictively cramped city site on the south side of Chicago, and is consequently long and narrow in plan with its elaborate entry not presented to the street, but on its southern side. It is among a small number of early Wright houses, which are sometimes typified as a "monitor," meaning a third, small story is added above the main projection of the eaves with its own hipped roof. In the Heller house, the third story is elaborated by being only partly enclosed, and having a heavy sculptured frieze of draped figures by Richard Bock. Bock was an Oak Park sculptor, who collaborated with Wright on his house and studio complex at Oak Park, providing the striking sculptural decoration of the facade of the studio, and worked on many of Wright's later commissions. Most notable of these was the Susan Lawrence Dana house at Springfield, Illinois, of 1902–1904, the most elaborate and complex of Wright's Prairie houses, and the huge Larkin administration building of 1903. The street facade of the Heller house is made conspicuous by Bock's richly sculptured panels, and the elaborately columned and decorated porch, which supports the roof.

It appears that Bock was happy to work from Wright's designs, and Wright was so pleased with the plaster panels of the Heller house that he was to incorporate some of the panels into his drafting room in Oak Park. The inset porch with its florid fillagree decoration and sills wide enough to support plant pots is a curiously Sullivanesque extravaganza that appears out of place on such a comparatively modest building in a city setting. At this period Wright was not able to exercise much control on his client's wishes, and the house

RIGHT: Side elevation. Constructed on a long, narrow city lot, the entrance to the house is not on the street facade, but on the southern side. The house is distinguished by its smaller third story, which is only partly enclosed, forming a loggia with its own hip roof. This feature is sometimes known as a "monitor," and here it is constructed of the same yellow Roman brick with stone dressing as the rest of the house, but with the addition of some extraordinarily elaborate sculptured decoration.

as it stands may have represented a particular desire of the client for such an elaborate public statement. Other portions of the exterior elevation are embellished with a deep paneled frieze of a design, which might be termed Arabic in derivation, while the columns marking the entrance to the house are Romanesque in origin, the whole forming an extraordinarily eclectic design mix. The house is constructed of yellow Roman brick with white stone dressing, and the interior materials consist in the main of waxed white oak, and plaster in a rough sand finish that appears saturated with pure color.

As one of the earliest of Wright's three-storied residences, the Heller residence is of interest as a link in development between the so-called "finished attics" of the earliest work, and the fully evolved Prairie Style. Together with the W. Irving Clark house of 1893, which has a third floor ballroom on its front elevation, the Heller house anticipates a design seen later at its most complex and complete in the Frederick C. Robie residence of 1906. The disposition of its internal spaces might also be said to look forward to the design of the mature Prairie house. The main living spaces on the ground floor, including the dining room and living room are of the cruciform shape, which was to be developed into one of the main features of the fully evolved Prairie designs. In part, however, this might be explained by the restrictions imposed by the site and Wright's ingenious response to it.

LEFT: Detail of decoration of the frieze of the third story. Decorative panels by the sculptor Richard Bock form a frieze along the loggia, where they are protected from adverse weather by the deep overhang of the eaves. This was Bock's first collaborative venture with Wright, and was adapted from a design by Wright for a privately printed edition of John Keat's poem *The Eve of St Agnes*. Bock appears to have turned Wright's original static male figures into draped female dancing figures, which are more appropriate to an architectural relief.

RIGHT: Detail of third-story elevation. The sculptured loggia, which forms the third floor of the Heller house, is in distinctive contrast to the plain, rather austere facade as a whole. It features figures in high relief by the sculptor Richard Bock, who was to work with Wright on many projects, including his own home and studio. The sculptured capitals in Romanesque style are reminiscent of the floriated decoration seen in many buildings by Louis Sullivan, including the Auditorium building and the trading room of the Chicago Stock Exchange.

E. ARTHUR DAVENPORT HOUSE

Constructed: 1901
Address: 559 Ashland Avenue, River Forest, Illinois 60305.

The Davenports were prominent citizens of River Forest, and both were active in community affairs. E. Arthur Davenport, who worked all his life with the Pulman Company, was River Forest's first township supervisor, while Mrs Susan Davenport played an important part in River Forest life by holding the post of president of the River Forest Women's Club. Wright's design for the Davenport's home was intended as a statement of their social standing. It is also one of the few examples of a building that reflects Wright's one brief formal partnership with another architect, Webster Tomlinson, for a period of barely 12 months between February 1901, when the design for the house was apparently completed, and some time after March 1902. It would seem that Webster Tomlinson had nothing to do with the design of the buildings, but handled the commissions and contracts of the business as a managing partner.

The original design for the Davenport house would seem to have conformed almost exactly to "The Small House with Lots of Room in It," which was published under Wright's name in *The Ladies' Home Journal* of July 1901. This was part of an enterprising plan by Edward Bok, the Head of the Curtis Publishing Company, to acquaint the public with progressive design and improve what he saw as the low level of contemporary domestic buildings. The campaign to sell complete sets of contemporary architect's working drawings to readers of the popular magazine at five dollars a set met with much opposition from architects. They were

RIGHT: Main facade with entrance porch on left. Both the main roof and the porch have low, broad gables with a pronounced overhang and stained board-and-batten siding. When the house was originally built, it had a front verandah and a different window treatment for the dining room but this was changed soon after it was built. The geometric design of the windows and ribbon development of the casements on the upper floor enhance the verticality of the design.

dismayed at such an unconventional method of disseminating their work, and also by stipulations laid down by Bok, such as replacing the Victorian "parlor," and all that this implied, with a "living room," a new concept in the period. Wright had no reservations about accepting the invitation to submit designs, as he shared Bok's reformist ideas, and saw the readers of *The Ladies' Home Journal* as ideal consumers of his work in a time of unprecedented demand for domestic design. The revolutionary designs did not have the immediate impact that had been hoped for, although this was to come later. Itemized costs were included with each design bought by the readers, and "A Small House with Lots of Room in It," which was to be built for $5,800, appears to have been taken up in local commissions immediately under Wright's control, as with the Davenport house.

The house is cruciform in plan with small wings on each side, and originally had a verandah on the front elevation. The modest house was surfaced with board-and-batten siding, and had particularly fine glass; a key component in Wright's early work. When the house was remodeled the original glass was reused. The employment of clear and milk glass in a simple yet elegant rectilinear design with cames (an electroglazing technique that holds the glass in place) of varying thickness, gives the whole design a lightness and modernity unusual in Wright's work at the time.

The gables of the design of the Davenport house mark it as a transitional work in Wright's career, he quotes *The Ladies' Home Journal* article to explain their inclusion: "the average home-maker is partial to the gable room...The gables in this design are slightly modeled, making the outlines 'crisp.'"

The interior planning of the house perfectly exemplifies Wright's revolutionary ideas. An explanation of these ideas accompanied the publication of the drawings: "The plan disregards somewhat the economical limit in compact planning to take advantage of light and air and prospect, the enjoyable things one goes to the suburbs to secure...The dining room is so coupled with the living room that one leads naturally into the other without destroying the privacy of either."

ABOVE: Living room. The Davenport house is similar in design to Wright's later published plans for "A Small House with Lots of Room in It," although the customized details are finer than those specified for the budget model houses. The space here, though not extensive, is made to seem larger by the rectilinear treatment of the walls and especially by the extensive windows. The design of the windows affords privacy in the geometric design of the art glass casements and frame.

RIGHT: Living room fireplace and inglenook. As befits a house of modest size, albeit one whose architect's plan was for a home "with Lots of Room in it," the inglenook space is scaled down from the grandeur of such commissions as the Winslow house. The hearth is of simple brick and flagstone, although the space is clearly differentiated, and subtly lit.

FRANK W. THOMAS HOUSE

Constructed: 1901
Address: 210 N. Forest Avenue, Oak Park, Illinois 60302.

The Frank Thomas house may be regarded as Oak Park's first Prairie Style residence. It was the first of the houses that were to transform domestic design and create new models for living, both in the United States, and through publication across a worldwide market. It marks a distinctive break with Wright's earlier houses in the suburb. Several of the more conventionally designed houses are located nearby, and the studio facade of Wright's own residence is on Forest Avenue.

Like other Prairie houses, the house is characterized by its long, low lines, which are perfectly integrated into its site, and in Wright's own words "all unnecessary heights have...been eliminated, and more intimate relation with outdoor environment sought to compensate for loss of height." As with other early Prairie houses, it is set on an unprepossessing suburban site for which Wright compensated by concentrating on what he termed the "vista within," achieved in this case by some of the most spectacular art glass ensembles of his entire career. Much of the success of the early Prairie designs lay in their "exotic" use of space and light, the "breaking of the box," which was a move away from the traditional compartmentalization of living spaces, and to their sympathetic use of natural materials. These radical features distinguished them from contemporary domestic buildings, as well as the complex entryways, so characteristic of Wright's work of the period.

RIGHT: Entrance vestibule doors and windows seen against the light. Wright's idea of an apparently continuous flow of space in which the walls seem to vanish is achieved in the form of a shimmering light-diffusing screen, which also helps ensure privacy. The entire glass ensemble, which is formed of doors, screens and electric light fittings uses opalescent glass, gold leaf and mother-of-pearl applied in varying degree to the stylized geometric forms. The squares and bars of opalescent glass form a shimmering screen of almost unbroken light so that the walls seem to disappear. Stylized forms of feathery wheat crown the design of the upper parts of the windows and doors of the vestibule.

Few entryways are more complex than that of the Thomas house, which is reached by ascending two flights of stairs. The visitor is then made to change direction to discover the entrance door, which is hidden from the street. By doing so, Wright is controlling the visitor's reaction, encouraging them to experience the building's spatial dimensions, before entering it. The design sets up their expectation of what might await them once they enter the interior.

Wright's conception of glass used as a continuous shimmering screen is realized in spectacular fashion in the entrance vestibule. His idea of a continuous flow of space in which the walls seemingly vanish is here achieved by what appears as an almost unbroken band of glass. Here it takes the form of a light-diffusing screen, which also helps ensure privacy. The spectacular space is realised by Wright's working partnership with the glassmakers Giannini and Hilgart, a successful collaboration between designer and makers, which was to stand Wright in good stead for several of his most famous later commissions. The

LEFT: Exterior elevation from the stair leading to the vestibule of the garden entrance. A complex entryway is characteristic of many of Wright's houses, few however are more complex than that of the Thomas house, which is reached by ascending two flights of stairs through a maze-like structure which raises visitors' expectations, especially as they are made to change direction to discover the entrance door which is hidden from the street. Wright controls the visitor's reaction, encouraging them to experience the building's spatial dimensions before entering and setting up their expectation of what might await them once they gain the interior. The extraordinary art glass designs are echoed by the staircase decoration and the original entrance light.

ABOVE: Entrance facade. The main entrance to the house is clearly indicated at ground
level with an entrance archway; the only curved form to be seen on the facade. The long,
low lines of the house, which is built on an L-plan, are complemented by the extensive
terraces and the shallowness of the rooflines. The house is further distinguished by the
ribbon development of the casement windows with their sparkling art glass, which give
a vertical emphasis to the whole.

electroglazing process, and the specialist skills of Giannini and Hilgart are evident in the use of opalescent glass, gold leaf, and mother-of-pearl applied in varying degrees to the stylized geometric forms. As with other Prairie houses, the glass designs evoke formalized ears of wheat and other prairie forms, and the continuous bands of art glass help reinforce the horizontality of the overall design, while the vertical lines of the arrow-head glass motifs help provide a necessary balance.

The Frank W. Thomas house is generally considered to be Wright's first truly evolved Prairie house, and its appearance was considered startling at the time. It formed a contrast to the historicism of the neighboring Nathan Moore house, for example, whose owner had been so upset by the modernity of the Winslow house of 1893 that he had insisted on having "nothing but an English House," meaning one in Tudor style. As Nathan Moore had not wished to court controversy in the design of his home, it appears that the original owners of the Thomas house moved out after a very short time. The house became locally known as "The Harem," a term still in use today, and a measure of the criticism leveled at it and its architect at the time. Four years after it was built a visiting architectural critic expressed the common view: "The neighbors called it "The Harem", and it does have a sort of seraglioic appearance, quite Oriental in its high encompassing blank walls… That sort of thing is simply exotic."

Within a very short time Wright was to refine the Prairie concept first seen in the Thomas house, and produce a series of masterpieces of the genre, culminating in the Robie house of 1910, completed at the end of a decade spent in perfecting the Prairie Style.

RIGHT: Detail of exterior light on the stair leading to the vestibule. The light is seen against the background of the vestibule glass, which is particularly remarkable. Such survivals of exterior lights are a rarity, and would have been very unusual at the time when electric light in domestic buildings was expensive and confined to those who could afford a generator.

UNITY TEMPLE

Constructed: 1905
Address: 875 Lake Street, Oak Park, Illinois 60302.
Guided and self-guiding tours available.

Wright's major public building of his years in Oak Park was the Unity Temple, a major commission for the small studio in 1905, and one that still stands as a key building in the history of Western architecture. The Unitarian-Universalist congregation, whose wooden church had been destroyed in a storm in 1905, had a modest budget of some $45,000 with which to build, and this necessitated the use of economic building materials. The solid masonry of concrete decided upon was turned to brilliant effect, during construction between 1906 and 1909, both in the esthetics of the design and the practical need for a peaceful space on what was then a heavily trafficked site. Wright himself saw Unity Temple as a watershed in his career. Interviewed some 50 years after it was built, he reflected: "I think that was about the first time when the interior space began to come through as the reality of that building. When you sat in Unity Temple, you were sitting under a big concrete slab but your eyes go out into the clouds on four sides. There were no walls with holes in them."

Wright conceived the Temple as a cube and "a noble form of masonry." The overhead structure is carried on four hollow concrete posts, which enables the walls to be non-supporting, and to thereby act as screens. This is an effect further enhanced by the band of light screens immediately below the roof, forming a

RIGHT: View of the interior looking towards the pulpit. Unity Temple is in fact a complex of three spaces, the "worship space," shown here, Unity House, the parish space to the south which is used for social and educational purposes, and a central entrance hall. The space used for religious services, the "Temple" shown here gives its name to the whole structure and is the only public building of Wright's early career to be still in use. The eye is directed straight to the magnificent coffered skylights, which form the entire ceiling. Of amber and beige glass and in a pattern of squares and rectangles, each is set at a different angle to the whole.

clerestory, or "clearstory" as was used to light the interiors of churches, and cathedrals in medieval Europe. From the outside none of this is made apparent, and the visitor is confronted with a fortress-like building, monumental in conception, unabashedly modern in its material construction, and with fully integrated ornament, all of concrete.

Concrete is an ancient building material, used by the Romans to construct their most monumental buildings, such as the Colosseum and the Pantheon in Rome. The Romans used poured concrete for economy of means, and rapidity of construction across its vast empire, as the process used whatever local materials were available in its aggregate. Surfaces could be faced with finer materials to give the grandeur and monumentality so essential to the finished result. Unity Temple's surfaces represent one of the key tenets of modernism, that of "truth to material." Of major importance in Wright's career, these surfaces represent the first experiment with what was to be a 55-year fascination with "the gutter-rat" of building materials as he called it. A material that he would mold to become the perfect medium for the expression of his extraordinary ideas, from the series of houses built in the 1920s, known as "California Romanza," to his crowning achievement in the public sphere, the Solomon R.Guggenheim Museum in New York City.

The building has three functional spaces: Unity Temple itself, used for religious services; Unity House, the Parish house; and between both an entrance hall. The low ceiling of the hall, in typical Wrightian

RIGHT: View of the exterior. The poured concrete used for the construction produces a fortress-like structure, an appearance which also recalls ancient temples and one that is perfectly in keeping with the function of the building. At the same time the solid nature of the concrete walls shuts out the noise from the busy main street site, which in Wright's day was much greater even than today. The distinctive concrete ornamentation of the columns is fully integrated into the design, and the monumental building expresses both a powerful modernity and the temple's clear links to ancient religious structures.

fashion, raises the visitor's expectations of the interior to come, while providing a sense of sanctuary. Wright's use of art glass throughout the building, but especially in the top lighting, and in the side alcoves, was intended, as he himself wrote: "to get a sense of a happy cloudless day into the room...daylight sifting through between the intersecting concrete beams, filtering through amber glass ceiling lights. Thus managed, the light would, rain or shine, have the warmth of sunlight."

ABOVE: Detail of Unity Temple facade. Seen in close-up, the nature of the concrete forms that make up Unity Temple are clear, especially as they are unfaced, or as Wright himself termed it "left as themselves with no facing at all.' The blocks are hollow, and contained heating ducts to ensure the warmth and comfort of the congregation.

ABOVE: View of facade. The references to ancient temple structures, and the idea of sanctuary, is clearly seen in this view as is the "closed" nature of the structure to the busy street. The repeating shapes of the columns and masses of the blocks is explained by the nature of the material of construction. Concrete was cast in wooden molds and as this was the chief item of expense, it was both functional and esthetically pleasing to repeat the forms. This gives Unity Temple an extraordinary sense of harmony, symmetry, and balance both outside, and within.

GAZETTEER

ROBERT G. EMMOND RESIDENCHOUSE

Constructed: 1892
Address: 109 S. Eighth Avenue, La Grange, Illinois 60525.

This is one of several early domestic designs that was commissioned while Wright was working out his five-year contract with Adler and Sullivan. Wright classified the commissions as the "bootlegged houses," because they were done while he still worked for, and was influenced by, Sullivan. The Emmond house, like the other houses of this period were, he said, "buildings all characterized to a certain extent by the Sullivanian idiom, at least in detail."
The Emmond house shares the same square plan with the Thomas H. Gale and Robert Parker houses in Oak Park, although it stands on a larger lot and has the addition of octagonal bays at its corners, which render it distinctive. Internally, its plan is conventional, and its living spaces are compartmentalized. It has a reception room, dining room, and a large central library area that opens from the terrace.

LEFT: Known as one of the "bootleg" designs, the house is a plain-frame structure built on a modest scale to a conventional plan shared with other "bootleg" houses of the period. The design is distinguished by the polygonal forms of the corner bays with extensive windows, and by the tall, steeply sloped roofs.

THOMAS H. GALE HOUSE

Constructed: 1892
Address: 1027 Chicago Avenue, Oak Park, Illinois 60302.

Although it shares a very similar plan with both the Robert G. Emmond residence and the Robert Parker residence, the houses differ in detail. As with the house built for Thomas' brother, Walter, a block away, the rooms are disposed in what might be seen as a conventional, Victorian fashion, without the flow of interior space, described as "breaking the box," which is so characteristic of Wright's later work. As in the other houses of this period, the entryway opens directly onto the street, without the subtleties of design that distinguish the entrance to Wright's own house in Oak Park, built the same year. All three "bootleg" houses were also originally sided with clapboarding, and have been altered by subsequent owners. The Thomas H. Gale house is distinguished by its corner polygons with comparatively large window areas, and its tall polygonal roof line.

RIGHT: This clapboard house is another "bootleg" commission that bears a strong resemblance in both plan and elevation to both the Emmond residence at La Grange, and the house built for Thomas' elder brother Walter at Oak Park of the same year. The design might be described as an exercise in an abstract Queen Anne manner.

ROBERT P. PARKER HOUSE

Constructed: 1892
Address: 1019 Chicago Avenue, Oak Park, Illinois 60302.

The Parker house is similar in plan and elevation to the Thomas H. Gale house, and that of his brother Walter Gale, which are both neighboring houses on Chicago Avenue. Its square plan also mirrors that of the Robert Emmond residence of 1892 at La Grange. As with these other "bootlegged" designs (a term used to describe the unauthorized commissions Wright undertook, while serving his five-year apprenticeship with Adler and Sullivan), which were all built within a remarkably short time, it is the customized detail that distinguishes one from another. Basically the house is an exercise in the Queen Anne style so fashionable at the time. However, the sharp lines of the turreted roof, and the window treatment of the Parker house might be said to anticipate Wright's later rectilinear style.

LEFT: As with the Walter Gale and Thomas Gale residences, built at the same time and also on Chicago Avenue, this is an exercise in the Queen Anne style. This is particularly evident in the design of its elevation, although the sharp rectilinear form of its window design, and the detailing of some of the interior features may be said to anticipate Wright's later work.

WALTER M. GALE HOUSE

Constructed: 1893
Address: 1031 Chicago Avenue, Oak Park, Illinois 60302.

Like other "moonlighted" designs, such as the neighboring house built for Walter Gale's
younger brother, Thomas, a block away, the Walter Gale house has little about it that would
suggest the radical directions Wright's work was to take later in the same year. It does not even
reflect the innovations already present in his own house on Chicago Avenue. The house has a
plain-frame structure, which can be seen to offer a practical solution to designing a small-scale
family home of the time. Its most distinctive external feature is a two-story semi-circular bay,
adjacent to a long, thin dormer, which also rises through two stories. Internally, the plan is a
conventional one that has distinctly
compartmentalized living spaces.

RIGHT: Like the neighboring house on Chicago Avenue built
for Walter's younger brother, Thomas, and several other
"bootleg" houses built at the same period, the rounded forms are
reminiscent of the currently fashionable Queen Anne style. The
house is distinguished by its dormer window with pargeting
(decorative motifs cut into the rough plaster) that rises through
two stories.

PETER GOAN HOUSE

Constructed: 1893
Address: 108 S. Eighth Avenue LaGrange, Illinois 60525.

This modest house may well have been the last of Wright's "moonlighted" designs, worked on while he was chief draftsman at the firm of Adler and Sullivan. Such "moonlighting" broke the terms of his five-year agreement, and caused the rift with Louis Sullivan, his architectural mentor. As with the other "bootleg" houses, as they are known, there is very little that is radical in the exterior design. The plan of the house is remarkably conventional in its layout and the living spaces are distinctly compartmentalized. Wright was unknown at the time and was not able to assert his radical ideas with his clients. The facades use broad shingles and stucco for decorative and functional effect, and originally there was a porch running the entire length of the entrance facade.

LEFT: View of the main facade today. Wright's original design included a wide porch that ran the entire length of the facade. In early photographs, it enhanced the horizontal lines of the facade. The original shingle siding, and stucco decoration have also been altered. It appears that because of a disagreement between Wright and the original owners, the house had to be completed by another architect.

ROBERT W. ROLOSON ROWHOUSES

Constructed: 1894
Address: 3213-3219 Calumet, Chicago, Illinois 60616.

The four Roloson rowhouses, or apartments as they are sometimes known, represent a unique commission in Wright's early work. Essentially, they are four separate apartments, linked by their party walls, and each designed on the mezzanine principle around a top-lit stairwell that extended through all four floors of the interior. After a fire in 1981, the interiors were gutted, and all that remains of Wright's original work is the exterior. The facades are the most distinctive feature of the houses, and an extraordinary and unique exercise in a form that Wright was never to repeat. Four huge gables, set side by side, top a severely geometric facade formed of square motifs, and mullioned windows, reminiscent of English Tudor architecture yet markedly modern in form.

RIGHT: View of the main facades showing the four distinctive gables that form the most striking features of the exteriors of the apartments, and the panels of wall decoration in the manner of Louis Sullivan. Each of the apartments is self contained with its own entrance, and has spacious dimensions of some 3000 sq. ft. (278m²).

CHAUNCEY L. WILLIAMS HOUSE

Constructed: 1895
Address: 530 Edgewood Place, River Forest, Illinois 60305.

Chauncey Williams, one of Wright's earliest clients, was part of Wright's circle, sharing many interests with the architect. This may explain some of the freedom allowed Wright in the design, particularly of the dormers (which were remodeled after 1900), the tall brick chimneys, and the octagonal dining room and library. Oriental influences, not least the stone river boulders set into the brick work of the entry, are also characteristically Wrightian, emphasizing an organic unity with nature. From family accounts it would appear that the river boulders were gathered by the Wright, Williams, and Waller families on outings to the Desplaines River. They were incorporated into the building to signify its unity with the indigenous landscape; an early example of this key aspect of Wright's later work.

LEFT: View of entrance facade. The house is unusual in Wright's work of the time, particularly in its dormers and use of materials. The use of Roman brick and stucco is distinctive, as are the steeply pitched roofs, and the octagonally shaped dining room and library. The bedroom dormers were to be remodeled by Wright to provide better ventilation.

NATHAN G. MOORE HOUSE

Constructed: 1895, remodeled 1923
Address: 333 Forest Avenue, Oak Park, Illinois 60302.

The Moore residence is the only black-and-white house of Wright's career, designed as such because the client would "have nothing but an English house," meaning a half-timbered structure evoking England's Tudor past. It was a building style of great popularity in Victorian England. Wright produced a typically idiosyncratic variation on the Tudor theme, using a lot of half-timbering, and incorporating a steeply pitched roofline. The house was gutted by fire in 1922, and rebuilt to Wright's design, in part from the first floor up. In the rebuilding, Wright dramatically heightened the roofs, and enlarged the chimney stacks, giving the house a startlingly vertical emphasis, offset by the terraces and patterns of the half-timbering.

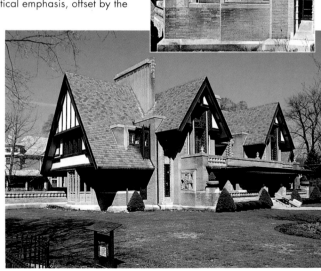

ABOVE AND RIGHT: Side elevation and porch. The porch of the original 1895 design was a more modest structure, although of roughly the same dimensions. The 1922 remodeling of the house after the fire enlarged and elaborated many of the original "Elizabethan" features of the house, but the decorative motifs of the porch decoration are an eclectic mixture. The detail here draws on both Sullivan and Tudor strap-work decoration.

ROMEO AND JULIET WINDMILL

Originally constructed: 1896
Address: Spring Green, Route 23, Taliesin, Wisconsin 53588.

Wright built the original 60ft. (18m) high windmill to supply water to Hillside Home School, which was run by his maternal aunts, Jennie and Ellen Lloyd Jones. The windmill is composed of interlocking diamond and octagonal forms, which combines symbolic form (the Shakespearean lovers, Romeo and Juliet) and function. It may also be seen as an arrangement of Wright's favorite Froebel forms; the simple irreducible geometric shapes of the wooden blocks given him in his childhood by his mother. As such, the Froebel shapes might be said to be particularly appropriate to a co-educational school run on progressive lines. Wright said of the tower, "each is indispensable to the other...neither could stand without the other. Romeo, as you will see will do all the work and Juliet cuddles alongside to support and exalt him. Romeo takes the side of the blast and Juliet will entertain the school children."

RIGHT: The windmill was built to pump water to the Hillside Home School run by his aunts, Jennie and Ellen Lloyd Jones, and Wright was later to characterize the windmill as "my first example of engineering architecture." The structure uses geometric forms, reminiscent of Wright's childhood education where he was introduced to Froebel blocks. It contained an observatory, and later a loudspeaker to relay music to the surrounding countryside.

HARRY C. GOODRICH HOUSE

Constructed: 1896
Address: 534 N. East Avenue, Oak Park, Illinois 60302.

The house was the thirteenth to be completed by Wright in the Oak Park and River Forest areas in a remarkably short space of time. It marks a transitional style, away from Wright's experiments with fashionable historical modes, such as the Tudor style gables of the Roloson rowhouses, or the Colonial style of the Blossom house. The Goodrich house is more strictly geometrical in its design, and has strong horizontals that anticipate the Prairie houses to come, and marked triangular emphases throughout the design of the facade. The windows of the second story, which contain art glass, are positioned directly beneath the steep overhang of the eaves. These provide protection from the extremities of the Oak Park climate—shade from the glaring sunlight of the summer, and shelter from the harsh snows of the winter. The plan of the house is a progressive variant on the neighboring Charles E. Roberts house, and has a centralized hearth, separate dining and sitting rooms, and a library.

LEFT: View of the entrance facade. The strong geometric elements of the design are much in evidence in this view, not only in the diamond shapes of the decoration of the facade, but also in the steep pitch of the roof. This is enhanced by the broad overhanging eaves, and the caming of the art glass, second-story windows.

ROLLIN FURBECK HOUSE

Constructed: 1897
Address: 515 Fair Oaks Avenue, Oak Park, Illinois 60302.

The Rollin Furbeck house has some resemblance to the Heller house of the previous year particularly in its lofty elevation, which has open loggias to the north and south together with a large porte-cochere. The decoration of the columned loggias is markedly influenced by Sullivan's use of ornament, and the low flanking roofs have widely jutting eaves. However, the central, three-story facade, contains features that make this a significant transitional work in Wright's early career. Both living and dining rooms have a range of picture windows, and the third floor probably contained a range of rooms for servants, which were unusually spacious for the time. The spacious brick-built porch, which is large enough to be termed a porte-cochere, is remarkable both for its size, and the intricate brickwork of its piers.

RIGHT: View of the front elevation. The Rollin Furbeck house features a square plan with a central feature rising through three stories, the columned porches recall those of the Heller house of the year before. The picture windows of the living and dining rooms are a new feature in Wright's houses.

GEORGE W. SMITH HOUSE

Constructed: 1898
Address: 404 Home Avenue, Oak Park, Illinois 60302.

The design for the Smith house bears a resemblance to plans for low cost housing submitted to an early client of Wright's, Charles E. Roberts, chairman of the Board of the building committee of Unity Temple in 1896. As far as is known, none of the schemes for such houses were built, but Wright was to adapt the principles in a modest design such as this. As with other early designs, the facade uses shingle siding rather than Wright's later board-and-batten siding, which was used in Prairie designs, and in the 1950s, low-cost Usonian designs. The house has steeply pitched roofs, and deeply overhung eaves, which were in their original state made of shingles stained red. These must have given the house a distinctly Japanese appearance; an early example of Wright's use of a major influence on his later work.

LEFT: View of the main facade. The modest dimensions of the house and the shingle siding are characteristic of other early Wright designs, although the living room windows are of unusual size. This, together with the steep, pagoda-like roofs give the house its distinctive character.

EDWARD R. HILLS HOUSE

Constructed: 1900, 1906
Address: 313 Forest Avenue, Oak Park, Illinois 60302.

The spacious Hills residence (known since its restoration in 1977 as the Hills-DeCaro House after its then owners) marks an advance in design on earlier houses. In some respects it is similar to other Oak Park houses of the same period. It has a striking entry porch, for example, however this is placed on the northeastern axis and leads the visitor left, by way of a spacious entrance hall, to living and dining rooms, and a handsome stairwell. The house was occupied by the Hills family for 45 years, but was damaged by fire in 1976. Much of the original built-in furniture by Wright, together with fine art glass, survived the fire, and the house itself has been meticulously restored.

RIGHT: View of entrance facade and porch. The porch is set asymmetrically on the facade, and balance and harmony are achieved by the geometric lines of the extensive windows and steeply pitched roofs. The porch roof echoes the geometry of the design of the main roof, while the rectangular horizontal motifs of the facade decoration, and caming of the art glass windows are balanced by the verticals of the porch pillars, and the impressive chimney stack.

WALLIS SUMMER HOUSE

Constructed: 1900
Address: 3407 S. Shore Drive, Wisconsin 53115.

Henry Wallis owned land on Lake Delavan, Wisconsin, and sold plots, through his real-estate business, to Oak Park residents such as himself who wanted a holiday home. Wright's design for the summer house is based on a module of 39in. (99cm), and is an early instance of his use of the unit system, later to be used in Prairie house designs, and the Usonian houses. The original design was a precursor of Wright's design for a "fireproof house for $5000," which was to be published in *The Ladies' Home Journal* of April 1907. This design has been obscured by later extensions, and refaced with asbestos shingles, and cedar stained in the original dark green.

ABOVE: View of the main front of the building. The original two-story building was built on a 39in. (99cm) module, and was a simpler structure with a porch and terrace opening from the central living space. Later extensions and enclosures have obscured the original design.

WILLIAM G. FRICKE HOUSE

Constructed: 1901
Address: 540 Fair Oaks Avenue, Oak Park, Illinois 60302.

The Fricke house is spacious in design, and has a projecting dining room bay, and a larger projecting living room with the emphasis on Wright's quintessential "sacred hearth." Bedrooms and servants' rooms are housed in three stories, beneath projecting eaves. The major living spaces surround a central hall that leads from the entrance. The house is stucco-faced, which gives it a monumental appearance, and in this respect it might be seen as a precursor to Unity Temple, although the materials of its construction are different. The block-like facade, which has a three-story central elevation and a projecting living room has its marked horizontality balanced by the pronounced vertical elements of the window design and the stepped lines of the whole facade. Internally the house is distinguished by its detailing and by the fact that it retains much of Wright's original fixtures and fittings.

ABOVE: Detail of exterior showing the wide overhang of the eaves that provides much needed shade, and the distinctive dark banding around the windows. The vertical elements of the window treatment are echoed in the art glass, and the wide banding balances the essentially horizontal lines of the design as a whole.

WARD WINFIELD WILLITS HOUSE

Constructed: 1901
Address: 1445 Sheridan Road, Highland Park , Illinois 60035.

The Ward Willits house represents a considerable progression in Wright's work. It is a move away from the eclectic mix of influences he was working through in the Tudor style Nathan Moore house, for example, or the experimentation with the Colonial style evident in the Blossom house. The house is long and low in design, and has symmetrical wings and sharply jutting eaves. The terraces and long low lines of casement windows, filled with sparkling art glass, are a new departure in his work. The interior spaces all center on a massive Roman brick "sacred hearth" as the focal point of a family home, and the flow and organization of the internal spaces demonstrates how Wright was well on his way to evolving a fully developed Prairie Style.

ABOVE: View of the side elevation. The house is an extended cruciform in plan, each wing branching out from a massive central hearth. Here the extensive overhang of the eaves shades the extensive glazing of the ground floor, and the large windows of the second-floor bedrooms.

LEFT: Living room exterior. The long, low lines of the house and its terraces are balanced by the vertical elements of the design of the art glass windows, which are sheltered at the upper level by the extraordinarily deep overhang of the eaves. The living room windows on the terrace side are ranged from floor to ceiling, the rectilinear design of the art glass throughout the house incorporates milk glass in its design.

WILLIAM E. MARTIN HOUSE

Constructed: 1902
Address: 636 N. East Avenue, Oak Park, Illinois 60302.

Similar to the neighboring Fricke Residence in some respects, notably in its elevation, this three-story house represents a marked development in Wright's ideas from the Fricke house, begun but a year earlier. William Martin was brother to Darwin D. Martin, and the family connection was to prove an important one for Wright's future. For the Martins, and their family connections, he was to build nine buildings. These included several houses, and the Larkin Company Building in Buffalo, now demolished, that was the first major business construction of his career. The Martin house is distinguished by a clearer and more coherent plan than Wright's other houses of the time, and by a design with an emphasis on the horizontal, enhanced by the extensive fenestration. The spacious interior includes a verandah opening from the dining room, as in the Ward Willits house, and some fine art glass, notably a hall skylight reminiscent of the work in Wright's studio complex. Originally the pergola, which was added in 1909 and since demolished, was the center of the composition, which included extensive landscaping.

LEFT: View of entrance facade. The Martin house may be seen as a development in Wright's work at the time, particularly with regard to the geometric elements of the facade, and the use of glazing. The facade rises through three stories yet remains markedly horizontal in form, and the extensive range of fine art glass windows are all rectilinear in design.

ROOKERY BUILDING REMODELING

Constructed: 1905
Address: 209 LaSalle Street, Chicago, Illinois 60604.
Open to the public during business hours.

The Rookery building, an early skyscraper by Burnham and Root constructed in 1888, contained the offices of both Wright and his client William H. Winslow, and was managed by another important early client, Edward C. Waller. The offices of the American Luxfer Prism Company were also in the building. The Luxfer Prism system was a radical invention in the days before the widespread use of electric lighting, as it helped refract natural light into commercial interiors. Wright's work for the company provided him with the means to build his own architectural practice at Oak Park, and make much needed extensions to his family living space. Wright remodeled the interior of the Rookery as one of his first public commissions, contributing the light court and entry. Subject to an extensive recent restoration, the atrium faithfully reproduces Wright's design, demonstrating his innovative use of metals (both in the structure and light fittings), and marble.

RIGHT: Interior view of the light court and lobbies. The grand mezzanine staircase, and white planters at the base are of white marble. Other elements of the Wrightian design include the light fixtures, and the intricate patterning of the marble surfaces with an incised gold-leaf design.

INDEX